FAIRACRES PU

LENT WITH
GEORGE HERBERT

TONY DICKINSON

SLG
Press

© 2022 SLG Press
First Edition 2022

Fairacres Publications No. 194

Print ISBN 978-0-7283-0327-0
Fairacres Publications Series ISSN 0307-1405

Edited and typeset in Palatino Linotype by Julia Craig-McFeely

*Biblical citations are from the King James Version of the Bible throughout, unless
otherwise noted in the text.*

The edition of the poetry by George Herbert was created for this publication
from the first edition of *The Temple: Sacred Poems and Private Ejaculations*,
(Cambridge: Thomas Buck, 1633), British Library C.58.a.26.

SLG Press
Convent of the Incarnation
Fairacres • Oxford
www.slgpress.co.uk

Printed by
Grosvenor Group Ltd, Loughton, Essex

CONTENTS

—◆—

—◆—

For Malcolm Lesiter

PREFACE

I cannot now remember when George Herbert first came into my life. Probably, as for many people of my generation, it happened in the school assemblies at which we sang 'Teach me my God and King' or 'The God of love my shepherd is' or 'Let all the world' to Basil Harwood's splendid tune, 'Luckington', a good bellow for teenage boys, especially when the first verse is repeated, as it sometimes is, at the end of the hymn. I do remember picking up a copy of the 1967 Faber publication, *A Choice of George Herbert's Verse*, edited and introduced by R. S. Thomas. That would have been early in my university career, and it sufficiently 'spoke to my condition' for me to add a second-hand copy of the 1908 Everyman edition of *The Temple* and *A Priest to the Temple* (otherwise *The Country Parson*) to my library a few years later. That edition had an introduction by another poetical Thomas: Edward. I also remember being reduced almost to tears as I read 'Love bade me welcome' in the course of a para-liturgical celebration when I lived in Durham.

So, when Malcolm Lesiter, my training incumbent, gave me the responsibility of producing three short Holy Week addresses for the people of All Saints, Leavesden, in the mid-1980s, I took the opportunity of sharing something of my enthusiasm for George Herbert's poetry by devoting each evening, from Monday to Wednesday, to one stanza of 'The Agonie', beginning with 'Philosophers have measured mountains ...' and ending with 'Who knows not Love ...' Those talks form the basis of this book's treatment of that poem and may explain why that chapter is rather longer than the others.

Other chapters, or parts of chapters, including the Introduction, were originally sermons preached in various places during the course of the past three decades on 27 February, the day when the Church of England's Calendar commemorates George Herbert. The detailed commentary on most of the other poems is mainly based on talks given as part of a Lent course that took place at St Francis' church in High Wycombe earlier this century. The commentary on 'Easter' is an expanded revision of the sermon that was preached at the dawn Eucharist that Easter morning. In 2019 all of the talks were revised and updated to be given as Lent Lectures in Genova. They were part of the 'Spirituality Series' within a broader project, *English Voices in Genoa*, hosted by the Church of the Holy Ghost, where I currently serve as chaplain. At each stage of this long process, and with each revision, I have discovered new aspects of Herbert's gift for articulating the life of the Spirit in words that are simple on the surface but which conceal within them, as I have tried to show, shades of meaning through which Herbert paints, as his friend Nicolas Ferrar recognized, 'the picture of a divine soul in every page', or, perhaps more appropriately, given Herbert's love for and skill in music, 'such a harmony of holy passions as would enrich the world with pleasure and piety'.

TONY DICKINSON

LENT WITH
GEORGE HERBERT

INTRODUCTION

George Herbert was buried in St Andrew's Church, Bemerton on 3 March 1633, exactly a month before his fortieth birthday. He was well-connected socially, being kin to the Herbert Earls of Pembroke. He was also connected poetically: his mother was a friend of another of the great Anglican poet-priests, John Donne, Dean of St Paul's, and George's older brother, Edward, Lord Herbert of Cherbury (1583–1648), was a minor poet and lay theologian of considerable accomplishment. During the four decades of his life George Herbert had been, variously, scholar, courtier, translator, musician; but finally, and above all else, poet and, for the last period of his life, parish priest of Bemerton, in Wiltshire, at that time a village on the banks of the Avon a mile or so from Salisbury and now one of the city's western suburbs. He was a man who 'lived and ... died like a saint, unspotted of the world, full of alms-deeds, full of humility, and all the examples of a virtuous life'. That, at least, was the opinion of his first biographer, Izaak Walton (1593–1683), who knew many of George Herbert's friends and recorded for posterity their memories of Herbert's life.[1]

George Herbert was Rector of Bemerton for less than three years. The story of his brief ministry there is told by Walton in his 'The Life of Mr. George Herbert'. During that time he and his household lived in such a way that he was to become for Anglicans the ideal of the faithful English country parson, much as, two centuries later the curé of Ars-en-Dombes, Jean-Baptiste

---

[1] Izaak Walton, *The Life of Mr. George Herbert* (London: Tho. Roycroft, 1670). Reprinted in Izaak Walton, *The Lives of Donne, Wotton, Hooker Herbert and Sanderson* (London, William Pickering, 1827), 247ff. Citations are from this edition.

Vianney, was to become the ideal of the French Catholic parish priest. To provide himself with guidelines for his work in Bemerton and a set of targets to aim at, George Herbert wrote *The Country Parson*, sometimes known as *A Priest to the Temple,* a handbook of pastoral care that was first published in 1652, nearly twenty years after the author's death. This classic account of parochial ministry is still read, and its insights still used (or as some critics have argued, abused), today.[2] The reflections that are contained in *The Country Parson* provide, in many ways, a commentary on some of the poems explored here.

George Herbert lived at a time of great changes: in religion, in political life, in the human view of the world in which we live. More and more was being discovered about the physical universe. As he wrote:

> Nothing hath got so far
> But man hath caught and kept it as his prey;
> His eyes dismount the highest star;
> He is in little all the sphere;
> Herbs gladly cure our flesh, because that they
> Find their acquaintance there.[3]

Herbert clearly shared in the excitement at these discoveries. He was as aware as anyone of the pleasures that the world could offer. He had been a courtier, and a prominent figure in the life of the University at Cambridge, impressing King James I when, in his role as Public Orator, he welcomed the king to the city. The transition from Cambridge to Bemerton was the outcome of a serious struggle and disappointed hopes. Izaak Walton alludes to the long delays and doubts that went before

---

[2] See Justin Lewis-Anthony, *If You Meet George Herbert on the Road, Kill Him: Radically Re-Thinking Priestly Ministry* (Bloomsbury Publishing, 2009).

[3] 'Man', lines 13–18.

Herbert's decision to take holy orders. Herbert knew himself thoroughly: few have conveyed so succinctly the sheer repetitive tedium of sin as he does in 'Sin's Round'. Our constant cycle of failure is reflected in the very structure of the poem, expressing the way in which human futility takes its victims round and round in circles.

But it was out of the raw material of his own spiritual struggles that Herbert produced some of the finest religious poetry in the English language. A few of his poems are well-known today among English-speaking Christians as hymns. Among the best-known are: 'Teach me, my God and King', 'Let all the world in every corner sing', 'King of glory, King of peace' and Herbert's metrical version of Psalm 23, 'The God of love my shepherd is'. C. H. H. Parry and Benjamin Britten set individual poems. Ralph Vaughan Williams set poems by Herbert for baritone, chorus and orchestra under the title *Five Mystical Songs*. One of those settings, 'The Call', is also used sometimes as a hymn.

That relationship to music goes deep. The antiquary John Aubrey (1626–1697), who was related to Herbert's wife Jane, tells us that George Herbert was a skilled lutenist (as was his brother Edward) and a composer who set his own poems, although sadly none of those settings has survived.[4] As for the poems themselves, Walton tells us that during George Herbert's last illness his great friend Nicolas Ferrar, the founder of the Christian community at Little Gidding dedicated to spiritual discipline and social service, sent a member of that community, Edmund Duncon, to find out how Herbert was. As Duncon was preparing to leave Bemerton, Herbert gave him the manuscript collection of his poems, with these words:

> Sir, I pray deliver this little book to my dear brother Farrer, and tell him, he shall find in it a picture of the many spiritual

---

[4] John Aubrey, *Brief Lives: A Modern English Version*, ed. Richard Barber (Boydell Press, 1975), 137ff.

conflicts that have past betwixt God and my soul, before I could subject mine to the will of Jesus my master; in whose service I have now found perfect freedom. Desire him to read it; and then, if he can turn it to the advantage of any dejected poor soul, let it be made public; if not, let him burn it; for I and it are less than the least of God's mercies.[5]

Fortunately for English-speaking Christians, Nicolas Ferrar's opinion of the manuscript was favourable. Indeed, he commented that 'There was in it the picture of a divine soul in every page; and that the whole book, was such a harmony of holy passions, as would enrich the world with pleasure and piety'.[6]

Herbert's poetry weaves together recognition of the glory and diversity of God's creation, and of the ingenuity of human beings in their attempts to map and control that creation; awareness of human frailty and sinfulness, of how far each one of us falls short of the divine glory; and awed realization of the infinite love of God, displayed most fully in what God has done for humanity in Jesus Christ, and made freely available to all through the sacrament of Holy Communion. These great themes (relevant as much to the twenty-first century as to the seventeenth) are expressed in language that often appears direct and simple, but whose simplicity frequently conceals a depth and density of meaning that few writers can match. Human frailty and God's infinite mercy and forgiveness are subjects that dominate Herbert's poetry.

> Yet through the labyrinths, not my grovelling wit,
> But thy silk twist let down from heav'n to me
> Did both conduct and teach me how by it
> To climb to thee.[7]

---

[5] Walton, *Lives*, 309.

[6] Ibid.

[7] 'The Pearl', ll. 37–40.

That 'silk twist', the thread by which Herbert climbs, is God's self-revelation in Jesus of Nazareth. Even in the midst of our most determined efforts to ignore Him, God gently but insistently calls us to love and serve Him.

Herbert never presumes on God's love. His poems are both love-poems and prayers. Like any lover, he is conscious of his own unworthiness of the object of his love, only infinitely more so, because the object of his love is God, the God whom every English clergyman of that age knew to be 'one living and true God, everlasting, without body, parts, or passions; of infinite power, wisdom, and goodness; the Maker, and Preserver of all things both visible and invisible'; for that was how God is described in the first of the *Articles of Religion* to which every clergyman of that age had to subscribe.[8]

But in spite of his unworthiness, in spite of his sin and failure, in spite of the immense distance between the lover and the object of his love, George Herbert knew that he was loved in return. Indeed, that his being loved was the only thing that made it possible for him to love. The initiative, the marvellous, mysterious, unutterable initiative, is all on God's side. God searches us out. He seeks continually to draw us to himself, to welcome us as guests at His own table. We may know our unfitness for such an honour, but that is no obstacle to God. In the notes that he wrote for his own guidance as parish priest at Bemerton, George Herbert uses this love of God for His creation as a powerful argument against those who, in the Calvinist-influenced parts of the Church of England of those times, doubted that they were among the elect and were tempted to despair.[9]

---

[8] *The XXXIX Articles*, Article I, 'Of Faith in the Holy Trinity', as printed in the 1604 edition of Book of Common Prayer.

[9] See George Herbert, *The Country Parson*, Chapter XXXIV, 'The Parson's Dexterity in Applying of Remedies'.

There we have the God whom Herbert serves, not 'battering his heart' (like John Donne's),[10] but, as in another of the poems that I consider below, calling from afar,[11] a 'still small voice' (1 Kgs 19:12) to which the only response possible is self-surrender in love to Love, as the creature turns from absorption in itself to adore the God who made it. As he lay dying, Herbert reflected that 'his life could not be better spent, than in the service of his master Jesus, who had done and suffered so much for him'.[12] Jesus was for Herbert the most complete, living expression of God's love. His name is 'deeply carved'[13] on the heart of those who respond to that love, love poured out to the uttermost, freely and for all, the love 'which my God feels as blood, but I as wine'.[14]

Jesu

JESU is in my heart, His sacred name
Is deeply carved there: but th'other week
A great affliction broke the little frame,
Ev'n all to pieces, which I went to seek:
And first I found the corner, where was *J*,
After, where *E S*, and next where *U* was graved.
When I had got these parcels, instantly
I sat me down to spell them, and perceived
That to my broken heart He was I *ease you*,
   And to my whole is *J E S U*.

---

[10] John Donne, *Holy Sonnets*, XIV.
[11] George Herbert, 'The Collar', line 35.
[12] Walton, *Lives*, 301.
[13] George Herbert, 'Jesu', line 2.
[14] 'The Agony', v. 3, line 6.

ASH WEDNESDAY

Lent

Welcome dear feast of Lent: who loves not thee,
He loves not Temperance, or Authority,
      But is compos'd of passion.
The Scriptures bid us *fast*; the Church says, *now*:
Give to thy Mother, what thou wouldst allow
      To ev'ry Corporation.

The humble soul compos'd of love and fear
Begins at home, and lays the burden there,
      When doctrines disagree.
He says, in things which use hath justly got,
I am a scandal to the Church, and not
      The Church is so to me.

True Christians should be glad of an occasion
To use their temperance, seeking no evasion,
      When good is seasonable;
Unless Authority, which should increase
The obligation in us, make it less,
      And Power itself disable.

Besides the cleanness of sweet abstinence,
Quick thoughts and motions at a small expense,
      A face not fearing light:
Whereas in fulness there are sluttish fumes,
Sour exhalations, and dishonest rheums,
      Revenging the delight.

Then those same pendant profits, which the spring
And Easter intimate, enlarge the thing,
      And goodness of the deed.
Neither ought other men's abuse of Lent
Spoil the good use; lest by that argument
      We forfeit all our Creed.

It's true, we cannot reach Christ's forti'th day;
Yet to go part of that religious way,
      Is better than to rest:
We cannot reach our Saviour's purity;
Yet we are bid, *Be holy ev'n as He.*
      In both let's do our best.

Who goeth in the way which Christ hath gone,
Is much more sure to meet with Him, then one
      That travelleth by-ways:
Perhaps my God, though He be far before,
May turn, and take me by the hand, and more
      May strengthen my decays.

Yet Lord instruct us to improve our fast
By starving sin and taking such repast,
      As may our faults control:
That ev'ry man may revel at his door,
Not in his parlour; banqueting the poor,
      And among those his soul.

It is typical of George Herbert that he begins this poem with a paradox; almost, it seems, a complete nonsense: 'Dear *feast* of Lent'! We could be forgiven for wondering if this is a misprint, on the grounds that everyone knows that Lent is a *fast*, but the poet knows what he is saying. In post-Reformation England there were massive and sometimes very ill-tempered debates about how much of the tradition inherited from the medieval Church and, through the medieval Church, from the earliest Christian centuries should be retained, and how much discarded. The treatise *Of Ceremonies*, which has stood at the beginning of the Book of Common Prayer since Archbishop Cranmer's Second Prayer Book of 1552, and Article XXXIV, 'Of the traditions of the Church' reflect something of these controversies.[15] In England, although fasting in Lent was enforced by law from the reign of Henry VIII to the reign of James I, there was the matter of the Church authorities issuing licences to eat meat.

In such a situation, the keeping of Lent could be seen as an imposition, the sort of rule-bound religion of which the Reformers and their followers had been so critical. By welcoming the season as an opportunity to celebrate, rather than as an imposition to be endured, George Herbert is both taking the debate onto a completely different plane and getting in a gentle dig at those who were passionate in their denunciation of such 'Romish' tendencies. 'Who loves not thee, He loves not Temperance, or Authority, But is composed of passion', there is, in other words, no discipline in their lives.

What is more, Herbert implies, they do not take seriously the Reformers' insistence on 'Scripture alone' as the basis for

---

[15] *The XXXIX Articles,* Article XXXIV, 'Of the Traditions of the Church', as printed in the 1604 edition of the Book of Common Prayer:

> … Whosoever through his private judgement, willingly and purposely, doth openly break the traditions and ceremonies of the Church, which be not repugnant to the Word of God, and be ordained and approved by common authority, ought to be rebuked openly, (that others may fear to do the like,) as he that offendeth against the common order of the Church, and hurteth the authority of the Magistrate, and woundeth the consciences of the weak brethren.

Christian living. 'The Scriptures bid us *fast*', so those who ignore this discipline are living unscripturally. And to those who insist that, while the practice of fasting may be scriptural, the observance of Lent is of human origin, he points out that anyone who belongs to a formally constituted body of people, be it a guild, a livery company, a town council, has to abide by its rules. So why will not those who are members of what some would still call 'the family of the Church' follow the guidance of their Mother?

This leads to a reflection on the relationship between 'Mother Church' and the individual believer and reminds us that there is nothing new under the sun. In an age when there was a tendency for believers to set up private judgement over traditional practice, George Herbert reminds his readers that the mark of true Christian living has always been love, worked out in the context of humility. 'The humble soul, composed of love and fear' (by which he means reverence and respect rather than terror or anxiety) 'Begins at home, and lays the burden there, When doctrines disagree.' He suggests that if believers have a problem with patterns of faith that have nurtured others down the ages, they need to look carefully at what it is that gives rise to the problem. To put it in modern terms, it may not be 'our stupid vicar' or 'the out-of-touch hierarchy' or even 'those reactionaries at the Vatican' who are the problem: it may be my own pride and overweening self-confidence that cause me to stumble. When it comes to criticising or rejecting customs that have rightly evolved through common practice ('things which use hath justly got'), then it is likely to be my problem rather than that of the Church.

> True Christians should be glad of an occasion
> To use their temperance, seeking no evasion,
> When good is seasonable.

Going without when it is appropriate is a good thing: but (and here there follows a very compressed and quite difficult argument) sometimes it is appropriate not to fast, and to follow the letter of the law is actually self-defeating.Herbert spells out more clearly what this means when he sets out in *The Country Parson* some guidelines for 'The Parson in his House'. There, among various housekeeping rules for vicarages, he lays down the basic principle that

> fasting days contain a treble obligation: first, of eating less that day than on other days; secondly, of eating no pleasing or over-nourishing things...; thirdly of eating no flesh... The two former obligations are much more essential to a true fast than the third and last, and fasting days were fully performed by keeping of the two former, had not authority interposed; so that to eat little, and that unpleasant, is the natural rule of fasting.[16]

In other words, a true fast is better kept in finishing off the leftovers (reheating yesterday's lamb chops, for example) than in poaching, say, a fresh salmon steak or grilling a newly caught mackerel. 'Be sensible' is the message, and not over-scrupulous. Herbert is speaking from his own experience: throughout his life he endured poor health, causing great anxiety to friends and family on more than one occasion. It is on the basis of his chronic illness that he is able to affirm 'it is as unnatural to do anything that leads me to a sickness to which I am inclined, as not to get out of that sickness, when I am in it, by any diet.'[17]

But for all that, in the next stanza Herbert becomes quite evangelical, and very much our contemporary in feeling if not in language, when he points out the health advantages of fasting. At some stage in his life he had read a Latin translation of the *Discorsi della Vita sobria* by the Padua-born writer Luigi Cornaro

---

[16] George Herbert, *The Country Parson*, ch. X, 'The Parson in his House'.
[17] Ibid.

(?1467–1566), who by following his own advice allegedly lived to be ninety-eight.[18] Herbert responded to Cornaro's treatise, which was written when he was a young thing of eighty-five (or possibly sixty-nine), with such enthusiasm that he translated it into English.[19] What he has to say about 'sluttish fumes, Sour exhalations, and dishonest rheums, Revenging the delight' is pretty well straight out of Cornaro, and could have been written by many modern-day nutritionists. We over-indulge or eat the wrong kind of food at our peril, as this generation is beginning, belatedly, to discover. A body-mass index that is on the high side, to say nothing of full-blown obesity, comes with a hefty price-tag in the form of health problems.

Then, as so often in George Herbert's poetry, there comes a dramatic change of course. So far the discussion has been at the level of custom and practice, or healthy eating. Suddenly we are back to Scripture and the keeping of Lent is anchored firmly in Jesus's forty days in the wilderness. 'It's true, we cannot reach Christ's forti'th day', not in the western Church, at any rate, where the fast is punctuated by six Sundays (because even in Lent, Sunday is always a 'little Easter'). However, the imitation of Christ, which is a recurring theme in *The Country Parson*, encourages us to make the effort. 'We cannot reach our

---

[18] There is some doubt about Cornaro's date of birth. In order to enhance the claims made on behalf of his dietary programme he seems to have at various points backdated his birth, which is variously given as 1464, 1467 and 1484; the latter would make him 82 at death and is perhaps the most likely to be genuine, because it is the date that appears in an official document in the Venetian state archives.

[19] Herbert's *A Treatise of Temperance and Sobriety* (Cambridge, 1634) is an abridgement and translation of the Latin version of Cornaro's *Discorsi* that had been made by the Flemish Jesuit Lenaert Leys (Leonardus Lessius) and published in Antwerp in 1613 as an addendum to Leys's own *Hygiasticon*.

Saviour's purity; Yet are we bid, *Be holy ev'n as He.'* This is the same challenge that is issued in the First Letter of Peter: 'as He which hath called you is holy, so be ye holy in all manner of conversation; Because it is written, Be ye holy; for I am holy.' (1 Pet. 1:15–16). That challenge echoes words of Jesus in the Sermon on the Mount: 'Be ye therefore perfect, even as your Father which is in heaven is perfect.' (Matt. 5:48). Again, the hope is not of making it into heaven on our own strength, but of encountering Christ on the journey as we go, 'in the way that Christ hath gone', like Saul on the way to Damascus, perhaps, or, more likely, the two disciples travelling to Emmaus (Luke 24:13–35). Similarly, the God who turns to His people in love and takes them by the hand and brings them to safety is to be found several times in the Psalms and the Prophets, while Jesus takes Peter's mother-in-law by the hand (Mark 1:31), as He takes Jairus's daughter by the hand (Mark 5:41, Luke 8:54), to heal and make whole.

Then, in the final stanza of Herbert's poem, all the argument, the debate, the sound advice is drawn together into one prayer, based on Isaiah 58, with its rebuke to those whose fasts are self-serving rather than serving God.

Is not this the fast that I have chosen? To loose the bands of wickedness, to undo the heavy burdens, and to let the oppressed go free, and that ye break every yoke?

Is it not to deal thy bread to the hungry, and that thou bring the poor that are cast out to thy house? when thou seest the naked, that thou cover him; and that thou hide not thyself from thine own flesh?

Then shall thy light break forth as the morning, and thine health shall spring forth speedily: and thy righteousness shall go before thee; the glory of the Lord shall be thy rearward.

(Is. 58:6–8)

So, finally, we realize what it means to welcome the *feast* of Lent,

By starving sin and taking such repast
As may our faults control:
That ev'ry man may revel at his door,
Not in his parlour; banqueting the poor,
And among those his soul.

LENT I

Sin's Round

Sorry I am, my God, sorry I am,
That my offences course it in a ring.
My thoughts are working like a busy flame,
Until their cockatrice they hatch and bring:
And when they once have perfected their draughts,
My words take fire from my inflamèd thoughts.

My words take fire from my inflamèd thoughts,
Which spit it forth like the Sicilian hill.
They vent the wares, and pass them with their faults
And by their breathing ventilate the ill.
But words suffice not, where are lewd intentions;
My hands do join to finish the inventions.

My hands do join to finish the inventions:
And so my sins ascend three stories high,
As Babel grew, before there were dissensions.
Yet ill deeds loiter not: for they supply
New thoughts of sinning: wherefore, to my shame,
Sorry I am, my God, sorry I am.

When George Herbert, a few days before died, sent the manuscript collection of his poems to his old friend Nicolas Ferrar, he
described it as 'a picture of the many spiritual Conflicts that have
past betwixt God and my Soul, before I could subject mine to
the will of Jesus my master, in whose service I have now found

perfect freedom'.[20] This poem in many ways encapsulates those 'spiritual conflicts' to which Herbert refers. Herbert was an accomplished musician. Izaak Walton tells us that,

> His chiefest recreation was music, in which heavenly art he was a most excellent master, and did himself compose many divine hymns and anthems, which he set and sung to his lute or viol: and though he was a lover of retiredness, yet his love to music was such, that he went usually twice every week, on certain appointed days, to the cathedral church in Salisbury; and at his return would say, 'That his time spent in prayer and cathedral music, elevated his soul, and was his heaven upon earth.' But before his return thence to Bemerton, he would usually sing and play his part at an appointed private music-meeting …[21]

Sadly, none of Herbert's settings survive, but musical references abound in his poems—not least in this one, whose title and whose form reflect the musical form of a 'round', which can be instrumental, or vocal, or a dance.

In his epic poem *La Comedìa* Dante Alighieri uses dance to illustrate the life of heaven.[22] He portrays the heaven of the sun as a round dance in which a double circle of 'the wise', great theologians and philosophers, from Solomon to Thomas Aquinas, express in their activity what Dorothy L. Sayers in her commentary on this passage calls 'the order and harmony in which all of the diverse manifestations of God's truth are here conjoined'.[23] A similar image can be found three centuries later in the poem, 'Orchestra, or a Poeme of Dauncing' by Sir John Davies (1569–1626) which uses the symbolism of the universal dance of creation to commend the same virtues of order and harmony.

---

[20] Walton, *Lives*, 309.

[21] Idem, 296.

[22] *Paradiso*, X–XIV.

[23] Dante Alighieri, *The Divine Comedy: Paradise*, tr. Dorothy L. Sayers and Barbara Reynolds, (Harmondsworth, 1962), 139.

It is part of a tradition that encompasses such carols as 'Tomorrow shall be my dancing day' and Sydney Carter's song 'Lord of the dance', that links the dance of God in creation to the dance of our redemption, picking up the Hindu devotion to Shiva Nataraja and translating it into Christian terms, as the image of the 'Lord of the [cosmic] Dance' is applied to Jesus.[24]

There is, however, nothing godlike in this 'round' of George Herbert's. 'Sin's round' is a cunningly-constructed poem. It reflects the form of a round dance or a rondo in that the last line of each stanza becomes the first line of the next stanza, and the last line of the entire poem is identical to the first, so that the whole thing goes round and round. So, if this *is* a dance, then it is a dance like the Charleston marathons of the last great depression, the kind of endless, pointless competition featured in the 1969 film, *They Shoot Horses, Don't They?*

The lines of the poem, like the poet's offences, 'course it in a ring', and a very different ring from the one that ends the poem, 'Hope', that precedes it in the collection. As a wedding ring is, to quote the *Common Worship* marriage service, 'a symbol of unending love and faithfulness, to remind [the couple] of the vow and covenant which they have made',[25] so *this* ring is a symbol of the struggle against sin that is, at the human level, unending 'until death do us part'. And the endlessness of the ring is displayed not only in the form of the poem but also in its contents, through which George Herbert offers a classical account of how sin works its way into and through human lives. He points out how sinful thoughts, if they are not checked, lead to sinful words, which then lead to sinful actions. To this he gives an additional twist, by noting the propensity

---

[24] See Peter D. Bishop, *Words in World Religions* (SCM Press, 1979), 11, 36–8.

[25] *Common Worship: Pastoral Services* (Church House Publishing, 2000), 109.

of sinful actions to give rise in turn to more sinful thoughts — and the round dance continues.

Like the dance marathon in *They Shoot Horses, Don't They?*, this dance is utterly destructive. The imagery in the poem is all about devastation and death. The cockatrice in the first stanza was a legendary monster that hatched from an egg laid by a cock and incubated by a toad. It was reputed to have the power to turn people to stone by looking at them, making it first cousin to the basilisk.

The 'Sicilian hill' of the second stanza is Mount Etna, which was unusually active in the early years of the seventeenth century, particularly from 1614 to 1624. That decade roughly coincided with the period of George Herbert's active involvement in the intellectual life of Cambridge, a period during which there was a constant stream of new scientific discoveries, feeding a growing curiosity about the natural world. During those years Etna was more or less constantly erupting from its northern and north-western flanks, producing, it has been calculated, more than a thousand cubic metres of lava. This, although George Herbert did not live to see its climax, was the precursor of half a century of ever-greater activity ending in the devastating eruption of 1669 that destroyed the city of Catania.

Finally, in the third stanza, the poet uses the image of the tower of Babel, *the* biblical symbol of human hubris leading to destruction and division, the 'dissensions' of Herbert's poem. Then we finally realize, if we have not already, that 'Sin's Round' is a *danse macabre*, a dance of death from which no human power is able to extricate itself. 'wherefore, to my shame, Sorry I am, my God, sorry I am.'

The poem is, all in all, a depressing analysis of the human condition, and one that rings true in the experience of most human beings unless they are so blinded by their own hubris, and so caught up in the endless cycle of thought, word and action, that they cannot recognize the truth of their situation. But this is not George Herbert's last word on sin and we are not to despair. By God's grace it is possible to break out of this destructive cycle. In the chapter of *The Country Parson* that deals with 'The Parson's Dexterity in Applying of Remedies', George Herbert offers these wise counsels:

> ... if he sees [any of his flock] nearer desperation than atheism, not so much doubting a God as that he is theirs, then he dives into the boundless ocean of God's love, and the unspeakable riches of his loving-kindness. He hath one argument unanswerable. If God hate them, either he doth it as they are creatures, dust and ashes, or as they are sinful. As creatures, he must needs love them; for no perfect artist ever yet hated his own work. As sinful, he must much more love them; because notwithstanding his infinite hate of sin, his love overcame that hate; and with an exceeding great victory, which in the creation [he] needed not, gave them love for love, even the Son of his love out of his bosom of love; so that man, which way soever he turns, hath two pledges of God's love, that in the mouth of two or three witnesses every word may be established: the one in his being, the other in his sinful being; and this as the more faulty in him, so the more glorious in God. And all may certainly conclude, that God loves them, till either they despise that love, or despair of his mercy; not any sin else but is within his love; but the despising of love must needs be without it. The thrusting away of his arm makes us only not embraced.

LENT II

The Collar

I struck the board, and cried, No more.
                              I will abroad.
   What? shall I ever sigh and pine?
My lines and life are free; free as the road,
   Loose as the wind, as large as store.
                  Shall I be still in suit?
   Have I no harvest but a thorn
   To let me blood, and not restore
What I have lost with cordial fruit?
                              Sure there was wine
         Before my sighs did dry it: there was corn
            Before my tears did drown it.
   Is the year only lost to me?
                  Have I no bays to crown it?
No flowers, no garlands gay? All blasted?
                  All wasted?
   Not so, my heart: but there is fruit,
                  And thou hast hands.
   Recover all thy sigh-blown age
On double pleasures: leave thy cold dispute
Of what is fit, and not forsake thy cage,
                  Thy rope of sands.
Which petty thoughts have made, and made to thee
   Good cable, to enforce and draw,
                  And be thy law,

> While thou didst wink and wouldst not see.
>   Away; take heed:
>   I will abroad.
> Call in thy death's head there: tie up thy fears.
>   He that forbears,
>   To suit and serve his need,
>   Deserves his load.
> But as I rav'd and grew more fierce and wild
>   At every word,
>   Me thoughts I heard one calling, *Child*:
>   And I replied, *My Lord*.

Izaak Walton's *Life of George Herbert* is, for the most part, hagiography, a commendation of a man whom he, like many, considered to be a saint. Sometimes, reading it, we may wonder, when Herbert refers in his last illness to 'spiritual conflicts', what on earth those conflicts could possibly have been. We have fewer illusions after we have read Herbert's poetry. Many of his poems are indeed poems of conflict, the expression of a will not yet subjected to that of Jesus his Master. 'Sin's Round', in both content and form, pictures the human condition as a dreary treadmill of failure, going round and round with (humanly speaking) no way out. 'The Collar' represents, perhaps, an attempt to break free; but possibly not in the direction we might expect after reading Walton's *Life*.

At first sight, this is a much simpler poem than 'Lent', or even 'Sin's Round'. It might even be read as straight autobiography, if that were possible with a poet of the early seventeenth century. This is Herbert frustrated with his life, frustrated with his chronic ill-health, frustrated with the sudden and complete disappointment of his hopes of advancement at Court. Izaak Walton tells us that:

In this time of Mr. Herbert's attendance and expectation of some good occasion to remove from Cambridge to court, God, in whom there is an unseen chain of causes, did in a short time put an end to the lives of two of his most obliging and most powerful friends, Lodowick duke of Richmond, and James, marquis of Hamilton; and not long after him, king James died also, and with them, all of Mr. Herbert's court hopes; so that he presently betook himself to a retreat from London, to a friend in Kent, where he lived very privately, and was such a lover of solitariness, as was judged to impair his health, more than his study had done. In this time of retirement, he had many conflicts with himself, whether he should return to the painted pleasures of a court life, or betake himself to a study of divinity, and enter into sacred orders? (to which his dear Mother had often persuaded him.) These were such conflicts, as they only can know, that have endur'd them; for ambitious desires, and the outward glory of this world, are not easily laid aside: but, at last, God inclined him to put on a resolution to serve at his altar.[26]

In his *Life* Walton relates this period of agonized indecision to George Herbert's poem 'Affliction'. It might equally well be linked to the plot of 'The Collar', but, as often with George Herbert's poetry, we find that a superficial simplicity hides surprisingly complex depths. The overall journey of the poem may be the same as the journey that Walton describes, from a sense of life as 'All blasted, All wasted' to an acknowledgement that the one whose voice he hears amid his wild ravings is 'my Lord'; but within that journey there are clues that give this poem a wider reference than the purely autobiographical. George Herbert uses irony and ambiguity to disclose depths of meaning in a way that carries echoes of the Gospel according to John as we remember that for Herbert, 'the chief and top of [the Country Parson's] knowledge consists in the book of books,

---

[26] Walton, *Lives*, 267–8.

the storehouse and magazine of life and comfort, the Holy Scriptures. There he sucks and lives.'[27]

This poem operates at more than one level. Even its title, 'The Collar', suggests a double meaning. In other words, this poem is about a restraint, like a dog's collar, or a horse's, something that hands over control of one to another. However it sounds almost identical to another word, 'choler'; in early seventeenth-century English a common alternative among educated people for 'anger' or 'wrath'. Certainly this *is* an angry poem, not only in its language, but also in its form, or lack of form. There is no regular pulse or metre in the first sixteen lines. They vary in length, in stress pattern; there is no regular rhyme scheme. It is not until we reach line 17, 'Not so, my heart...', that we begin to find some sort of pattern emerging, and even there the rhymes do not fall into a regular sequence and the lines can be as short as four syllables and as long as ten. Only at the very end, with the resolution of Herbert's frantic arguing, do we find a clear resolution of the verse into a couplet of eight and six syllables—the rhythm, in case we had not noticed, that goes by the name of 'Common Metre', the rhythm of those metrical psalms that were for three centuries the staple of English worship and which, in George Herbert's time had the sort of 'modern classic' status that the hymns and songs of Fred Pratt Green or Timothy Dudley-Smith, Graham Kendrick or Sydney Carter have today.

For those who encounter George Herbert's poetry only when they sing it as hymns this poem probably comes as a particular shock. 'Teach me, my God and King' it is not. It is violent and physical in its imagery and in its language right from the start. 'I struck the board...' And even when the first blast of fury and frustration has run its course, we are talking about cages

---

[27] George Herbert, *The Country Parson*, Chapter IV, 'The Parson's Knowledge'.

and ropes and skulls, about imprisonment and death, about the constraints of being human.

In many ways this poem has a surprisingly modern feel to it. How does contemporary society cope with a sense of frustration and futility? How does it respond to suggestions that part of the human problem is a lack of discipline? It does so in terms, I suspect, that are not much different from those of this poem.

> Recover all thy sigh-blown age
> On double pleasures: leave thy cold dispute
> Of what is fit, and not forsake thy cage,
>> Thy rope of sands.
> Which petty thoughts have made, and made to thee
> Good cable, to enforce and draw,
>> And be thy law,
> While thou didst wink and wouldst not see.

The first line-and-a-half, barring the versification, are a manifesto for the 'me' generation. They could have been written by anyone who thinks that the best remedy for being stuck in a dead-end job is a weekend on the lash; and the rest might easily have come from the pen of Richard Dawkins or the late Christopher Hitchens, arguing that God is a non-existent bogeyman whose self-deluded followers slavishly obey nonsensical and life-denying rules out of an irrational terror with which the adult has no truck. 'Call in thy death's head there: tie up thy fears'.

The irony is that it is the protagonist of the poem who 'winks and will not see'. In the midst of that outburst at the beginning of the poem there are a number of what can only be described as 'spiritual *doubles entendres*', words and phrases with are spoken in one sense, but can be interpreted (and are clearly *meant* to be interpreted) in another.

We might look again at the complaints made in the first half of the poem:

Have I no harvest but a thorn
To let me blood, and not restore
What I have lost with cordial fruit?
                        Sure there was wine
Before my sighs did dry it: there was corn
Before my tears did drown it.

'Restore what I have lost with cordial fruit' could be read quite literally, as the speaker intends it—but equally it could be read with reference to what Milton in the next generation would call 'man's first disobedience' in the garden of Eden, where human innocence and an intimate relationship with God are 'lost with cordial fruit', the fruit of the tree of knowledge of good and evil. That relationship is restored by the blood of Jesus, crowned with thorns by the mocking soldiers before they led Him away to His death.

For the Psalmist, corn and wine are signs of God's blessing (Psalm 4:7). Probably more to the point, it is 'grain once scattered in the fields and grapes once dispersed on the hillside'[28] that are reunited on the Lord's Table in the bread and wine of Holy Communion. Is that, one wonders, 'the board' that the speaker struck in his first outburst? The reality of this poem, at which the speaker 'didst wink and wouldst not see', is the spiritual reality, the Christian reality, that is ultimate reality. This is invisible to him in his rage, but it undercuts all his posturing and that will, in the end, tame him and bring him, so to speak, home.

It is this double vision that stops 'The Collar' from being, if it ever was, pure autobiography, and makes it applicable to us in our time as well as to George Herbert in his. It is this double

---

[28] *Common Worship: Times and Seasons* (Church House Publishing, 2006), 38. Based on *Didache* 9, otherwise known as The Lord's Teaching through the Twelve Apostles to the Nations (late first or early second century AD).

vision that enables us to see that it is the full-blown hedonism of the speaker, not freedom in Christ's service, that is a 'rope of sands', a rope that cannot provide a lifeline in time of trouble. The wild, rebellious egocentricity of the poem, with all its blustering, cannot, in the end, shut out the voice of 'one calling *Child*'. Nor can it prevent that resolution in an act of humble submission and faith, 'And I replied, *My Lord*', that betokens the subjection of the poet's will to that of Jesus his Master and the discovery that in His service there is perfect freedom.

LENT III

Sighs and Groans

O do not use me
After my sins! look not on my desert,
But on thy glory! Then thou wilt reform
And not refuse me: for thou only art
The mighty God, but I a silly worm;
   O do not bruise me!

O do not urge me!
For what account can thy ill steward make?
I have abus'd thy stock, destroy'd thy woods,
Sucked all thy magazines: my head did ache,
Till it found out how to consume thy goods:
   O do not scourge me!

O do not blind me!
I have deserv'd that an Egyptian night
Should thicken all my powers; because my lust
Hath still sew'd fig-leaves to exclude thy light:
But I am frailty, and already dust;
   O do not grind me!

O do not fill me
With the turn'd vial of thy bitter wrath!
For thou hast other vessels full of blood,
A part whereof my Saviour empti'd hath,
Ev'n unto death: since He died for my good,
   O do not kill me!

But O reprieve me!
For thou hast *life* and *death* at thy command;
Thou art both *Judge* and *Saviour*, *feast* and *rod*,
Cordial and *Corrosive*: put not thy hand
Into the bitter box; but O my God,
My God, relieve me!

The perspective on the poems provided by George Herbert's words as he handed over the manuscript to Edmund Duncon has freed us from one misapprehension about Herbert and his poetry: namely that the selection that has found its way into our hymn books represents the full range of his writing. That is, as we have seen, much more varied and complex in form and content than the gentle short-metre jog-trot of 'Teach me, my God and King' or the steady common metre of 'The God of love my shepherd is'. We have also broken away from the sense that George Herbert is some sort of gentle spirit, concerned only to praise and pray, watercolour by comparison with John Donne's dramatic and thickly laid-on oils. Nonetheless, it must be confessed that it *is* difficult to imagine George Herbert using the imagery and language of some of Donne's *Holy Sonnets*. A line like 'Spit in my face, you Jews, and pierce my side'[29] is inconceivable in a poem by Herbert.

Which is not to say that George Herbert does not do drama. There were enough fireworks in 'The Collar'. However, the drama tends to be internalized and to express perceived truth, rather than to show off. The poem 'Sighs and Groans' is a case in point. This poem, unlike 'The Collar', is one of those that have no obvious resolution. It begins as George Herbert pleads with God. It ends in the same way. This is, in one sense, a confession without absolution: but, like 'The Collar', it has a sub-text, an

---

[29] John Donne, *Holy Sonnets,* XI.

under-current, that surfaces in the final stanza to offer a hope that the surface of the poem does not.

'Sighs and Groans' is a poem rich in allusions to the Bible. Herbert draws on the law, the prophets, the Psalms, parables and Revelation as he builds up a picture of a human being in fear of God's judgement. Each plea resonates with echoes of Scripture but, as so often in George Herbert's poetry, there is a degree of ambiguity about how he means us to interpret them. The opening plea 'do not use me after my sins' echoes a verse from Psalm 103. The 'worm' at the end of the first stanza might point us to the 'worm and no man' of Psalm 22, but the plea with which that stanza ends, 'O do not bruise me!', suggests that it is more likely to link us to that other 'worm', the serpent of Genesis 3, who led Eve, and then Adam, astray and whose punishment is to experience the enmity of the woman's off-spring: 'I will put enmity between thee and the woman, and between thy seed and her seed; it shall bruise thy head and thou shalt bruise his heel.' (Gen. 3:15). This emphasizes the poet's humiliation and his sinfulness in terms that universalize it and links it with that 'original sin' that cast our first ancestors out of paradise.

The second stanza takes us into the New Testament, to St Luke's parable of the unjust steward (Luke 16:1–9), the one who squanders his master's resources or, as Herbert glosses it '… abus'd thy stock, destroy'd thy woods, Sucked all thy magazines …' (in this context magazines means storehouses, rather than glossy weeklies). Is it too much to interpret this in the contemporary terms of our laying waste to God's creation? 'My head did ache, Till it found out how to consume thy goods.' Again, the individual sin of greed is universalized so that humanity is under judgement for its misuse of the world's resources.

In the third stanza we return to the Hebrew Scriptures, to one of the plagues of Egypt:

And the Lord said unto Moses, Stretch out thine hand toward heaven, that there may be darkness over the land of Egypt, even darkness which may be felt. And Moses stretched forth his hand toward heaven; and there was a thick darkness in all the land of Egypt three days. (Ex. 10:21–22)

This is the 'Egyptian night' that arises from Pharaoh's hardness of heart and his refusal to let God's people go. Blindness is also, in the Gospels, a powerful symbol for those who refuse the light of Christ. In Matthew's Gospel Jesus calls the Pharisees 'blind guides' (Matt. 23.16, 24). John chapter 9 picks up this image, at the end of the account of the healing of the man born blind:

And some of the Pharisees which were with him heard these words, and said unto him, Are we blind also? Jesus said unto them, If ye were blind, ye should have no sin: but now ye say, We see; therefore your sin remaineth (John 9:40–41)

Similarly the clear reference to Adam in the lines 'my lust Hath still sew'd fig-leaves to exclude thy light' echoes John's words about Jesus as the light of the world, and his warning that,

… this is the condemnation, that light is come into the world, and men loved darkness rather than light, because their deeds were evil. For every one that doeth evil hateth the light, neither cometh to the light, lest his deeds should be reproved.

But he that doeth truth cometh to the light, that his deeds may be made manifest, that they are wrought in God. (John 3:19–21)

Not only do Herbert's words take us back to the man and the woman and their 'lust' for the fruit of the tree of knowledge of good and evil, they also point to the human inability to cope with that knowledge:

And the eyes of them both were opened, and they knew that they were naked; and they sewed fig leaves together, and made themselves aprons. (Gen. 3:7)

They hide from themselves. They hide from one another. They try to hide from God, who is light, and who formed humankind from the dust of the earth, dust to which human sin will ultimately return us all.

> In the sweat of thy face shalt thou eat bread, till thou return unto the ground; for out of it waſt thou taken: for duſt thou art, and unto duſt shalt thou return. (Gen. 3:19)

We are indeed 'frailty and already dust'. It is that frailty that has unfolded the prospect of punishment that so terrifies the poet, punishment which he imagines in apocalyptic terms. 'O do not fill me With the turn'd vial of thy bitter wrath', those 'seven golden vials full of the wrath of God' (Rev. 15:7), headlined by John the Seer as 'the seven last plagues; for in them is filled up the wrath of God' (Rev. 15:1). That mention of 'vials of … wrath' brings the poet back by a kind of free association to other vessels associated with God's anger, the bowls that were filled with blood when Moses struck the waters of the river Nile and Aaron stretched out his hand over the land of Egypt and

> upon their ſtreams, upon their rivers, and upon their ponds, and upon all their pools of water, that they may become blood; and that there may be blood throughout all the land of Egypt, both in vessels of wood, and in vessels of ſtone. (Ex. 7:19)

But this, in turn, leads Herbert on to reflect on the blood of Jesus, 'A part whereof my Saviour empti'd hath, Ev'n unto death' and to make the plea 'since he died for my good, O do not kill me!' And that leads to George Herbert's final, double-edged stanza with its plea for reprieve from the one who is 'both *Judge* and *Saviour, feast* and *rod, Cordial* and *corrosive*' (the emphasis is Herbert's). God is both the reward for which human beings long and the righteous one whom we fear because He calls our moral failures, our sins, into question. He is the medicine that makes us whole, but we can experience Him as either cordial, the medicine that does the heart good, or corrosive, the bitter medicine that acts by gnawing away at the seat of the disease.

It is at this point that we realize that, like 'The Collar', this poem is full of theological *doubles entendres*. All these things that the poet experiences as the corrosive wrath of God are equally the cordial that renews and strengthens the heart. It is not that we have been looking in the wrong place. We have been looking in the wrong way, through the wrong lens.

From the very beginning of this poem, we have been misinterpreting, or at best only partially understanding what God's purposes are. We have missed the point from the very first line: 'O do not use me after my desert', as we saw earlier, echoes Psalm 103, but the verse it echoes has a meaning totally contrary to the meaning that Herbert picks up. These words also echo the exchange between Polonius and the Prince in *Hamlet* II, ii. In the early seventeenth century *Hamlet* was regularly revived and frequently reprinted. Herbert may well have either seen it or read it.[30]

> He hath not dealt with us after our sins;
> > [that is, 'according to our sins']
> nor rewarded us according to our wickedness. (Ps. 103:10).

God's intention is plainly the opposite of what the poet fearfully anticipates. And so it is with the other images. The worm afraid of bruising is the worm who has been redeemed by Him who becomes for our sake 'a worm, and no man; a reproach of men, and despised of the people' (Ps. 22:6), and who is himself 'wounded for our transgressions' (Is. 53:5). The unjust steward receives his master's commendation rather than condemnation; because in the crisis caused by his bad management he acted shrewdly to secure a positive reception when he was dismissed

---

[30] I am grateful to Peter Whitfield for this insight.

from his post. The blind man receives his sight at the hands of God's Son, who has emptied His blood 'Ev'n unto death' to neutralize the vials of bitter wrath, who has 'died for [our] good'. This is the 'cordial' interpretation of this poem—a long way from the 'corrosive' that appears superficially. Human experience is necessarily ambiguous. We can interpret it as punishment from a wrathful, vengeful God, or as evidence that there is no God at all. Equally, we can penetrate beneath the surface of experience to discover there a God who is for us, who loves us, who works for our good, despite appearances to the contrary. This God not only knows our frailty. He has shared it in every respect, only without sin. He knows we are dust. And He loves us infinitely, even though we are less than 'the least of God's mercies.'[31]

---

[31] Walton, *Lives*, 309.

LENT IV

Redemption

Having been tenant long to a rich Lord,
   Not thriving, I resolvèd to be bold,
   And make a suit unto Him, to afford
A new small-rented lease, and cancel th' old.

In heaven at His manor I Him sought:
   They told me there, that He was lately gone
   About some land, which He had dearly bought
Long since on earth, to take possessiòn.

I straight return'd, and knowing His great birth,
   Sought Him accordingly in great resorts;
   In cities, theatres, gardens, parks, and courts:
At length I heard a ragged noise and mirth

   Of thieves and murderers: there I Him espied,
   Who straight, *Your suit is granted*, said, & died.

In understanding 'Redemption' a passage from the chapter in Herbert's book, *The Country Parson*, that deals with 'The Parson Catechising' is revealing:

> When once all have learned the words of the Catechisme, he thinks it the most usefull way that a Pastor can take, to go over the same, but in other words: for many say the Catechisme by rote, as parrats, without ever piercing into the sense of it.

Herbert's way of dealing with the catechism was rather different. He developed, what he called,

… an admirable way of teaching, wherein the Catechized will at length finde delight, and by which the Catechizer, if he once get the skill of it, will draw out of ignorant and silly souls, even the dark and deep points of Religion… the skill consists but in these three points: First, an aim and mark of the whole discourse, whither to drive the Answerer, which the Questionist must have in his mind before any question be propounded, upon which and to which the questions are to be chained. Secondly, a most plain and easie framing the question, even containing in vertue the answer also, especially to the more ignorant. Thirdly, when the answerer sticks, an illustrating the thing by something else, which he knows, making what hee knows to serve him in that which he knows not: As, when the Parson once demanded after other questions about mans misery; since man is so miserable, what is to be done? And the answerer could not tell; He asked him again, what he would do, if he were in a ditch? This familiar illustration made the answer so plaine, that he was even ashamed of his ignorance; for he could not but say, he would hast out of it as fast as he could. Then he proceeded to ask, whether he could get out of the ditch alone, or whether he needed a helper, and who was that helper.[32]

In this fifth of our poems, a sonnet entitled 'Redemption', there is an echo of Parson Herbert's method of catechizing.In her perceptive introduction to George Herbert's *Complete English Works*,[33] Ann Pasternak Slater suggests that in this poem, George Herbert is using the same technique that he used in catechizing the villagers of Bemerton. Here, in writing about redemption, Herbert is very clearly 'illustrating the thing by something else, which he knows, making what hee knows to serve him in that which he knows not'.

---

[32] George Herbert *The Country Parson*, Chapter XXI, 'The Parson Catechizing'.

[33] Ann Pasternak Slater, ed., *George Herbert, The Complete English Works*, Everyman's Library (Knopf, 1995).

Country people in seventeenth-century Wiltshire might have struggled, as many ordinary people today might struggle, with the concept of 'redemption', but most of them knew about tenancies and rent; and that is where George Herbert begins with the first half of the octet:

> Having been tenant long to a rich Lord,
> > Not thriving, I resolvèd to be bold,
> > And make a suit unto Him, to afford
> A new small–rented lease, and cancel th' old.

Many of Herbert's contemporaries would have recognized that scenario, as would many today. Family members may be firmly locked into 'generation rent'. One of the consequences of the COVID-19 pandemic has been a recognition of the predicament, not of farmers and agricultural workers, but of small, and some-times not-so-small, traders who have been caught by the termination of government reliefs that were available during lock-down and who are dreading the arrival of a rent demand that could easily drive them out of business. The remedy that has been suggested to some of them is the same remedy that the poet adopts: 'to be bold, And make a suit unto [the landlord], to afford A new small-rented lease.'

So far so straightforward. But as with much of George Herbert's poetry, there are subtle undertones for those who have ears to hear. Tenants not thriving and absentee landlords appear more than once in the writings of the prophets and the parables of Jesus. Those undertones begin to resonate a little more loudly in the second half of the sonnet's octet:

> In heaven at His manor I Him sought:
> > They told me there, that He was lately gone
> > About some land, which He had dearly bought
> Long since on earth, to take possessiòn.

Again, the biblical echoes are there for those who have ears to hear. When it comes to identifying this 'rich Lord', the fact that His manor is 'in heaven' is a big clue. We can almost hear Parson Herbert asking his flock, 'Who do you think the Lord in the poem is? Who lives in heaven? What land has He 'dearly bought on earth?' But Herbert does not give us time to answer those questions. At the beginning of the sestet, he moves the poem on:

> I straight return'd, and knowing His great birth,
>> Sought Him accordingly in great resorts;
>> In cities, theatres, gardens, parks, and courts:

As one would. Those were the very places where a poor man in the reign of James I or Charles I would expect to find an aristocratic land-owner relaxing after business—or even doing business. Again, might these lines also refer to another group of people who went searching for someone of 'great birth', and 'sought Him accordingly' in a king's court in a royal city, which turned out to be the wrong royal city? So, too, our searching tenant realizes that he is looking in the wrong place, and he extends the search. There is no friendly star to guide this seeker.

> At length I heard a ragged noise and mirth
>
>> Of thieves and murderers: there I Him espied,
>> Who straight, *Your suit is granted*, said, and died.

With everything but the bare bones hacked out of the story, it comes across as stark and senseless as a tavern brawl, like the playwright Christopher Marlowe's murder in Deptford in the year of George Herbert's birth, perhaps. But the hints beforehand have, to some extent at least, prepared us for this final couplet. As we hear the brief account of an apparently senseless death with its accompanying 'ragged noise and mirth Of thieves and murderers', we recognize Jesus, crucified between two

37

thieves; Jesus, in whose place the murderer Barabbas is allowed to go free; Jesus, mocked by the other condemned men as well as by the passers-by, who

> … reviled him, wagging their heads, And saying, Thou that destroyest the temple, and buildest it in three days, save thyself. If thou be the Son of God, come down from the cross. (Matt. 27:39–40)

and by the temple authorities,

> … the chief priests mocking him, with the scribes and elders, said, He saved others; himself he cannot save. If he be the King of Israel, let him now come down from the cross, and we will believe him. He trusted in God; let him deliver him now, if he will have him: for he said, "I am the Son of God". (Matt. 27:41–3)

So, if we have followed all the clues and asked all the right questions, we will have recognized the rich Lord as Christ and the poet as the representative of all humankind. We will have recognized, too, that the poet was granted the new lease he so desperately needed and that the grant was made at, and because of, Christ's death.

The catechist has done his work well. The telling of the story has enabled us to grasp it at 'gut level', at the level of our everyday experience. It has reminded us, too, in a way that the familiar words of the passion story sometimes cannot, of the extraordinary gulf between the 'rich Lord' and his miserable, undignified, apparently senseless death. This is Jesus who, as the writer to the Hebrews says, 'that he might sanctify the people with His own blood, suffered without the gate' (Heb. 13:12). He is taking His place with the outcast, the despised, the marginalized.

This is the 'new-made lease', the new covenant in Christ's blood that we celebrate every time we come together to share the bread and wine of Holy Communion. The 'rich Lord' suffers what Roman writers called, with searing contempt, 'the slaves' punishment'.[34] But what about 'th'old [lease]'? What was so difficult about that? Why did it cause the tenant 'not to thrive'?

For George Herbert the answer is clear. It is the old covenant, 'the law of commandments contained in ordinances' (Eph. 2:15), the law of which St Paul warned the Christians of Galatia:

> ... as many as are of the works of the law are under the curse: for it is written, Cursed is every one that continueth not in all things which are written in the book of the law to do them. But that no man is justified by the law in the sight of God, it is evident: for, the just shall live by faith. (Gal. 3:10–11)

It is faith that seeks out Christ crucified and discovers in His death the 'new-made lease', the covenant of grace, and discovers, also, that we ourselves and the rest of our over-busy, distracted world, are that 'land, which He had dearly bought Long since on earth,' the land whose price is His own life.

---

[34] Livy, *Ab Urbe Condita*, 24.14.7; Valerius Maximus, 2.7.12; Tacitus, *Historiae*, 4.11.3, among others.

LENT V

Love

Love bade me welcome: yet my soul drew back,
　　　　Guilty of dust and sin.
But quick-ey'd Love, observing me grow slack
　　　　From my first entrance in,
Drew nearer to me, sweetly questioning,
　　　　If I lack'd any thing.

A guest, I answer'd, worthy to be here:
　　　　Love said, you shall be he.
I the unkind, ungrateful? Ah my dear,
　　　　I cannot look on thee.
Love took my hand, and smiling did reply,
　　　　Who made the eyes but I?

Truth Lord, but I have marr'd them: let my shame
　　　　Go where it doth deserve.
And know you not, says Love, who bore the blame?
　　　　My dear, then I will serve.
You must sit down, says Love, and taste my meat:
　　　　So I did sit and eat.

When George Herbert in his last illness sent the manuscript of
his poems to his friend Nicholas Ferrar by the hand of Edmund
Duncon, it was not, as we might imagine, a sheaf of miscel-
laneous pages. In the Bodleian Library in Oxford there is a
manuscript whose first page carries a note identifying it as 'The
Original of Mr George Herbert's Temple, as it was first Licensed

for the press.'[35] Among scholars it is generally agreed that this is a fair copy of the original manuscript, a copy made by members of Nicholas Ferrar's community at Little Gidding and it is as certain as anything can be in this life that the first edition of George Herbert's poems, published in the year of his death, was printed from this document.

What the Oxford manuscript reveals is that the order of the poems was carefully shaped by George Herbert before he handed it on to Ferrar to see through the press. The poem we considered in the last chapter, for example, 'Redemption', is part of a sequence that runs from the next poem, 'The Agony' (which focuses on Jesus's prayer in Gethsemane), through 'Good Friday' and 'The Sepulchre' to 'Easter Wings'.

'Love' is the last poem in the main volume. It follows, appropriately, a sequence of poems that deal with three of the traditional 'four last things'. These are entitled 'Death', 'Doomsday', 'Judgement' and 'Heaven'. The fourth of those 'last things', 'Hell', has little place in George Herbert's thought, unlike some of his contemporaries, and the poems in which it appears tend to be early ones. Instead, in place of 'Hell' we find this poem, 'Love'.

This poem is the third with that title to survive into the final selection. There is a fourth that appears in a manuscript apparently written in Herbert's own hand about fifteen years before his death: but, for whatever reason, that did not make it to the final collection. The other two that did are printed together as 'Love I' and 'Love II'. They are both sonnets, cast in the same form as 'Redemption', and they are part of a sequence of poems that run from 'H[oly] Baptism', through 'Nature', 'Sin', 'Affliction' (the first of five poems with this title), 'Repentance', 'Faith', 'Prayer', 'the H[oly] Communion' and 'Antiphon', better

[35] Bodleian Library, Tanner MS 307, available online at digital.bodleian. ox.ac.uk/objects/fed4b4d1-8285-458f-8dad-2ba232f2f1a7/.

known, perhaps, from its first line, 'Let all the world in every corner sing'. Both 'Love I' and 'Love II', although they make use of a form very popular with poets of earthly love, are a protest against the identification of 'love' solely with sexual attraction. Herbert writes in 'Love I':

> Wit fancies beauty, beauty raiseth wit:
>> The world is theirs; they two play out the game,
>> Thou standing by: and though thy glorious name
> Wrought our deliverance from the infernal pit,
>
>> Who sings thy praise? Only a scarf or glove
>> Doth warm our hands, and make them write of love.

However, in 'Love II' he is even more critical of what he calls 'usurping lust'.

> Immortal Heat, O let thy greater flame
>> Attract the lesser to it: let those fires,
>> Which shall consume the world, first make it tame;
> And kindle in our hearts such true desires,
>
> As may consume our lusts, and make thee way.
>> Then shall our hearts pant thee; then shall our brain
>> All her invention on thine Altar lay,
> And there in hymns send back thy fire again:
>
> Our eyes shall see thee, which before saw dust;
>> Dust blown by wit, till that they both were blind:
>> Thou shalt recover all thy goods in kind,
> Who wert diseased by usurping lust:
>
>> All knees shall bow to thee; all wits shall rise,
>> And praise Him who did make and mend our eyes.

These two poems are, in a sense, polemical. They are attacking the view, widespread among poets of the early seventeenth century, that the only love worth writing about is erotic human love; and the boundary between human love and human lust is a blurred one, as a reading of George Herbert's contemporaries, the 'Cavalier poets', particularly Thomas Carew (1595–1640) and Sir John Suckling (1609–1641), reveals. 'Love' is very different. This is beyond partisanship, although it briefly refers back to the earlier pair. It represents the final resolution of 'the many spiritual conflicts that have passed between God and [George Herbert's] soul'.[36] For many it is simply 'Herbert's best poem'. Ann Pasternak Slater, in her commentary, refers to its 'translucent tone of chastened tenderness.'[37] A colleague told me some years ago: "'Love' is my 'desert island' poem, the one I would take with me."

In placing it right at the end of the collection, George Herbert is making a firm theological statement. This is what lies beyond death and doomsday. When the dusty traveller arrives at his final destination, he discovers that this is the essence of heaven.

However, as usual in George Herbert's poetry, this simply-worded poem, a dialogue between Love and the narrator, conveys a depth and complexity of feeling and thought. The initial image is of the narrator, weary and travel-stained, arriving at his destination. But underneath it lies a wealth of New Testament imagery. This dusty traveller is, perhaps, one of those dragged in off the streets by the great king's servants in the parable of the Great Supper in Luke's Gospel (Luke 14:16–24) or the Marriage Feast in Matthew's (Matt. 22:1–14). With Matthew's version in mind, and its account of the rejection of the man who lacked a wedding garment, it is hardly surprising that the narrator is hesitant about his likely reception. But this is Love, who offers not rejection but acceptance and welcome:

---

[36] Walton, *Lives*, 309.

[37] Ann Pasternak Slater, ed., *George Herbert, Complete English Works*, 488.

> ... quick-ey'd Love, observing me grow slack
> From my first entrance in,
> Drew nearer to me, sweetly questioning,
> If I lack'd any thing.

The warmth of the welcome, if anything, makes the poet feel even more uncomfortable, if not downright embarrassed, as his reply reveals: 'A guest, I answered, worthy to be here...'

At this point, we might turn to George Herbert's advice to the country parson included in his discussion of 'The parson in Sacraments':

> At the times of the Holy Communion, he first takes order with the Church-Wardens, that the elements be of the best, not cheape, or coarse, much lesse ill-tasted, or unwholsome. Secondly, hee considers and looks into the ignorance, or carelessness of his flock, and accordingly applies himselfe with Catechizings, and lively exhortations, not on the Sunday of the Communion only (for then it is too late) but the Sunday, or Sundayes before the Communion, or on the Eves of all those dayes. If there be any, who having not received yet, are to enter into this great work, he takes the more pains with them, that hee may lay the foundation of future Blessings. The time of every ones first receiving is not so much by yeers, as by understanding: particularly, the rule may be this: When any one can distinguish the Sacramentall from common bread, knowing the Institution, and the difference, hee ought to receive, of what age soever. Children and youths are usually deferred too long, under pretence of devotion to the Sacrament, but it is for want of Instruction; their understandings being ripe enough for ill things, and why not then for better? ... Thirdly, For the manner of receiving, as the Parson useth all reverence himself, so he administers to none but to the reverent. The Feast indeed requires sitting, because it is a Feast; but man's unpreparednesse asks kneeling. Hee that comes to the Sacrament, hath the confidence of a Guest, and hee that kneels, confesseth himself an unworthy

one, and therefore differs from other Feasters: but hee that sits, or lies, puts up to an Apostle: Contentiousnesse in a feast of Charity is more scandall then any posture.[38]

The poet's awareness of, and embarrassment at, his unworthiness is reflected in his response: 'I the unkind, ungrateful? Ah my dear, I cannot look on thee.' When we are confronted with the hurt we have done to someone we love, or who loves us, we turn away in embarrassment, unable to look them in the face.

But love makes us look. Love, the Creator, has given us the means to look, 'Who made the eyes but I?' If we look with love we see clearly. This is not the rose-tinted spectacles of sentimentality. This is the clear-eyed vision of unconditional love. We see not only the one we love, but ourselves. We recognize that we have marred what God has made and that this incurs guilt. This is the only time Herbert uses the word 'Lord' in this poem. He acknowledges, like the fourteenth-century Franciscan mystic Ramòn Llull (*c.* 1232–*c.* 1315/16), an unequal relationship between the Lover and the Beloved.[39] Herbert acknowledges his guilt and confesses his shame: 'let my shame Go where it doth deserve.' Presumably, if we pick up the thought of Matthew's parable (Matt. 22:13), it deserves to go into outer darkness. But love overrides both the shame and the guilt: 'know you not … who bore the blame?' This is love's atonement, the reconciliation brought about by Christ, of whom Peter wrote in his first letter that 'His own self bare our sins in His own body on the tree, that we, being dead to sins, should live unto righteousness: by whose stripes ye were healed.' (1 Pet. 2:24). At this point love triumphs. The one addressed as 'Lord' four lines earlier becomes 'My dear',

---

[38] George Herbert *The Country Parson*, Chapter XII, 'The Parson in Sacraments'.

[39] Ramòn Llull, *The Book of the Lover and the Beloved*, ed. Kenneth Leech trans. E. Allison Peers (Mahwah NJ: Paulist Press, 1978).

as the poet responds, no longer as the unworthy traveller, but as the unworthy lover of those courtly romances implicitly criticized by Herbert's other poems on 'Love', ready to serve the Beloved. In Christian terms, he is following the behaviour commended by Jesus in Luke 14:10 when He told diners who were squabbling over precedence at a banquet: 'When thou art bidden, go and sit down in the lowest room; that when he that bade thee cometh, he may say unto thee, Friend, go up higher.'

Even here, however, Herbert cannot escape the overriding power of love. *He* cannot serve. Love, as in Luke's Gospel and in John's, has already taken the lowest place. In the King James translation of Luke's Gospel, Jesus asks the twelve at the Last Supper, 'whether is greater, he that sitteth at meat, or he that serveth? Is not he that sitteth at meat? But I am among you as he that serveth.' (Luke 22:27). In John's Gospel He demonstrates this by taking the towel and the bowl and washing the disciples' feet, performing a task that was normally allotted to the most menial slave (John 13:2–17). 'You must sit down, says Love, and taste my meat'. The image comes, again, from St Luke's Gospel, where Jesus tells His disciples:

> Let your loins be girded about, and your lights burning; And ye yourselves like unto men that wait for their lord, when he will return from the wedding; that when he cometh and knocketh, they may open unto him immediately. Blessed are those servants, whom the lord when he cometh shall find watching: verily I say unto you, that he shall gird himself, and make them to sit down to meat, and will come forth and serve them. (Luke 12:35–37)

However, Love's words again have a double meaning. 'My meat' may be a simple echo of Luke 12:37, 'he shall gird himself, and make them to sit down to meat, and will come forth and serve them.' It may equally be that other meat that Jesus promises in chapter 6 of John's Gospel to those who believe in Him: 'that meat which endureth unto everlasting life, which the Son of man shall give unto you.' (John 6:27) The nature of that meat is explained more fully later in the same chapter when Jesus says:

> Whoso eateth my flesh, and drinketh my blood, hath eternal life; and I will raise him up at the last day. For my flesh is meat indeed, and my blood is drink indeed. He that eateth my flesh, and drinketh my blood, dwelleth in me, and I in him. (John 6:54–6)

This poem reminds us that it is not only at the end of life that we encounter infinite, unconditional love, but every time we gather at the Lord's Table to share in the communion of Christ's body and blood.

HOLY WEEK

The Agony

Philosophers have measur'd mountains,
Fathom'd the depths of seas, of states, and kings,
Walk'd with a staff to heav'n, and traced fountains:
    But there are two vast, spacious things,
The which to measure it doth more behove:
Yet few there are that sound them; Sin and Love.

Who would know Sin, let him repair
Unto Mount Olivet; there shall he see
A man so wrung with pains, that all His hair,
    His skin, His garments bloody be.
Sin is that press and vice, which forceth pain
To hunt his cruel food through ev'ry vein.

Who knows not Love, let him assay
And taste that juice, which on the cross a pike
Did set again abroach; then let him say
    If ever he did taste the like.
Love is that liquor sweet and most divine,
Which my God feels as blood; but I, as wine.

The first stanza of this poem reflects the way in which George
Herbert interpreted the huge expansion in human knowledge
at the beginning of the seventeenth century. When he speaks of
'philosophers', he includes under that heading some whom we
would think of as explorers or scientists, lawyers and political
commentators. 'Natural philosophy' embraced what are for us

distinct areas of study: among them mathematics, geography, biology, physics and astronomy. So Herbert's 'philosophers' include anyone engaged in increasing the sum of human knowledge. During his lifetime that sum increased dramatically. He was born at the end of the century of exploration that began with the voyages of Columbus and Vasco da Gama. The first years of his life overlapped with the last years of the English privateer-explorers, Drake, Hawkins and Frobisher. During the same period Galileo was carrying out the experimental work in physics and astronomy that was to bring him into conflict with Rome, while Johann Kepler and Tycho Brahe were also making observations that vastly expanded human awareness of the universe. Scholars in France, Italy and the Low Countries, were making discoveries in botany, mathematics and medicine. In England, as in other countries, there was a great outpouring of works about law, about political theory, and about history.

As Herbert reflected on these achievements in so many fields of human learning and discovery, he could truly say that 'Philosophers have... Fathom'd the depths of seas, of states, and kings, Walk'd with a staff to heav'n, and traced fountains.' For the first time in nearly two thousand years, and perhaps the first time ever, the feeling was growing that the world, indeed the whole universe, could be explored and explained. The operations of nature and of human society were open to study and investigation in a way that they had never been before.

At the same time as this huge explosion of knowledge was taking place there was a massive collapse of confidence. The new knowledge seemed to come at a terrible price, expanding so fast and changing people's outlook on the world in so many ways that it was positively frightening. Printed books, and the information they contained, were available to a wide public in a way that had never been possible when every volume had to be copied by hand. Furthermore, literacy was becoming more widespread, so people could read the books, and there were more people who had the income to pay for the books and the leisure time to read them. As a result, many felt that the new discoveries had damaged, if not destroyed, old certainties about the world and its Creator. Within Christian Europe, divisions over the interpretation of the Bible and the ordering of the Church caused conflicts whose effects are still with us five hundred years later. Even if we ignore the war between King and Parliament that broke out in England within half a dozen years of George Herbert's death, we should note that between his being elected a Fellow of Trinity College Cambridge in 1614 and his becoming Public Orator there in 1620, events in Prague sparked a conflict that was to engage continental European powers for the next thirty years, and devastate central Europe.

In our own age we have seen similar advances in scientific knowledge accompanied by religious and political turbulence. There has long been disquiet about the possibilities that biotechnology opens up; there is increasing anxiety about the opportunities for good and evil that exist in social media and the impact of artificial intelligence on many aspects of life. People are fearful and angry about the environmental impact of human actions. The desire for 'justice and peace' is now accompanied by a growing awareness of the need to respect the integrity of creation.

At the same time there is a mounting distrust of human beings' ability to order their relationships in such a way as to attain the goals of justice, peace and the integrity of creation, or to control the unpredictable and unwished-for results of scientific and technological advance. Orderly political life is under attack from without, by warlords, by terrorists, by single-issue pressure groups. It is subverted from within by a lack of accountability, by the putting of class or party advantage above the interests of society as a whole, by the corruption of those who hold power and authority and by the corruption of language. There are countries and regions where ordered civil government no longer exists and there are growing fears for the future of the western democratic tradition.

Three centuries ago, in the midst of this political turmoil and the immense expansion of knowledge of the world 'out there', George Herbert challenged his readers to re-examine two central aspects of our inner life that were, then as now, largely neglected, 'two vast, spacious things, The which to measure it doth more behove: Yet few there are that sound them; Sin and Love'.

Sin and Love. It is the conflict between those 'two vast, spacious things' that looms over the season of Lent and lies at the heart of our reflection and our prayer during Holy Week. 'Sin', that tiny word that covers so much human failure and self-ishness and misery and pain and horror, is brought up against that other little word 'love', four letters that stand for the infinite self-giving of God, creating and sustaining our world and all the other worlds of our universe. For Christians that self-giving is seen most clearly in the life of Jesus of Nazareth. As we reflect on his suffering and death, we see, perhaps, a key to under-standing how the conflict between sin and love is played out.

When George Herbert issues his invitation 'Who would know Sin, let him repair Unto Mount Olivet', the sin he has in mind is not just the moral failure of individuals. That is not the only sin we see in the story of the passion of our Lord Jesus Christ. That figure all alone in an agony of prayer in Gethsemane,[40] 'so wrung with pains, that all His hair, His skin, His garments bloody be', is struggling with sin on a cosmic scale. The cause of His agony as He contemplates the horror to come is not just Judas's treachery, Peter's cowardice, Pilate's desire for a quiet life, the sort of petty personal sin, the fear and desire for self-protection that prompts so many of the words and actions of which we are, in

---

[40] Cf. especially Luke 22:39–44.

our better moments, thoroughly ashamed. Those figures in the Gospels are, at this point in the story, a focus for something that has a cosmic dimension. In the actions of Judas and Peter and Pilate—and all the other actors in the story of Jesus's passion—we see not just their sins, or even our own sins. In them and in their actions we see, in summary, 'the sin of the world'.

If we follow the story to its end on Golgotha, we see that sin directing the actions of the Roman authorities, Pilate, and the execution squad, who live in a world recognizable to authority today. A world where all that matters in the end is having and hanging on to power, being in control, putting up a good front that will impress those who have greater power. It is a world where the lives of those with no power need not be taken into account and where their cries for justice can be safely ignored because the powerless are 'disposable'. To the values of *that* world Jesus said,

> The kings of the Gentiles exercise lordship over them; and they that exercise authority upon them are called benefactors. But ye shall not be so: but he that is greatest among you, let him be as the younger; and he that is chief, as he that doth serve. (Luke 22:25–6)

And so they killed Him.

We see that sin, too, influencing the behaviour of the Jewish leaders, the chief priests and the elders of the people, the religious establishment, highly educated, expert in the Law, and using their education and their expertise to control the lives of others. They had authority to say who was and who was not acceptable to God, to label others as 'in' or 'out'. That gave them status and they were stung by Jesus's message that, ultimately, it simply did not matter how well-educated people were, or how closely they kept the commandments of the Law; what *did* matter was the attitude of the heart towards God and towards others. The religious leaders could not cope when Jesus warned them that the dregs of society, the tax-gatherers and the tarts, were going into the kingdom of God ahead of the respectably religious (Matt. 21:31–2).

And so they plotted His death.

We can see that sin, too, in the disciples, our first ancestors in Christian faith. They forgot all that they had learned in their time with Jesus. According to Luke's Gospel, they were arguing about who was the greatest, even at the Last Supper. They forgot their promises of undying loyalty, of following Jesus to prison and death. According to Mark's Gospel, they all abandoned Him when He was arrested and ran away, saving their own skins— even if for one of them it meant losing his clothes (Mark 14:51–2). They could not even keep awake to give Him the support of their presence and their prayers in the garden at the foot of the Mount of Olives while He struggled with the knowledge of His approaching arrest and torture and death.

And so they *all* betrayed Him, not only Judas. They *all* denied Him, not only Peter.

'Who would know Sin, let him repair Unto Mount Olivet': or to Downing Street, or Westminster, the White House, the Kremlin: to the nuclear ruins in Chernobyl and Fukushima: to Yemen, awash with weaponry sold by the West: to the industrial-scale farms of the USA, the refugee camps of Lebanon, Turkey and Jordan. In each of those situations, as in others on every continent, folly or fear or greed or hatred is at work, corrupting and corroding God's image in human beings.

Human sin remains much as it was two millennia ago, although our greater power to affect the processes of nature and our greater mastery of means of destruction make the potential consequences much more disastrous. That solitary figure in the garden bears the weight of it all as He agonizes in prayer and struggles against a growing sense of being alone, cut off from all human contact; even, seemingly, at the end, in that terrifying cry from the cross, cut off from God. 'Sin is that press and vice, which forceth pain To hunt his cruel food through ev'ry vein'. Jesus is, as we might say, 'put through the wringer' at every level of His being. Nothing is left to Him.

That sense of nothingness, of total abandonment, is the end of sin, its terminal stage. Centred on self, sin in the end turns in on itself, away from the source of all life that is God and finds that at its centre there is simply nothing. Sin and evil are both parasitic upon what is good. They have no creative purpose and no ultimate reality in themselves. In one of his books Rowan Williams wrote about the people who carried out the massacre of six million Jews in Auschwitz, Belsen, Treblinka and elsewhere. In a memorable image he describes them as 'shadows spinning on the path to self-annihilation'.[41] Those who turn their backs so completely on the demands of God's love and His justice, even on the basic sense of belonging to the same species as their victims, are somehow no longer 'there' as human beings.

But, mercifully, God's love for His sinful creatures remains the same: unlimited, unending, totally, freely available to those who know their need of it and their dependence *on* it. Our task, during Holy Week, as we are exposed once more to the stark horror of the last hours of Jesus's life, is to look honestly at ourselves; to uncover areas of our lives in which we find ourselves turning our backs on God. Attitudes by which we share in the sin of the world; attitudes to power and privilege and status that make the world what it is; ways of thinking that find it easier to exclude others than to include them; weakness that puts personal gain or a quiet life ahead of any consideration of right or justice. If we can find the courage to admit these attitudes, this

---

[41] Rowan Williams, *Resurrection: Interpreting the Easter Gospel* (Darton, Longman & Todd, 1982), 21.

weakness, these ways of thinking, both to God and to ourselves, and if we can find the humility to accept our need for forgiveness both from God *and* from ourselves, then we can experience God's grace strengthening us to follow the way of the cross, the way that leads to the fullest expression of Divine Love.

As we follow the movement of George Herbert's poem from 'Sin' to 'Love', we move from the events of Maundy Thursday to those of Good Friday, from the Garden of Gethsemane to the horror of Golgotha. We witness the price that love has to pay for human failure and self-centredness.

> Who knows not Love, let him assay
> And taste that juice, which on the cross a pike
> Did set again abroach;

'That juice' is the heart-blood of Jesus, trickling down the shaft of the spear that, St John tells us, a soldier casually jabbed into the corpse 'just to make sure' (John 19:33–4). 'That juice' is the measure of God's self-giving for the world. God 'spared not His own Son, but delivered Him up for us all' (Rom. 8:32). The isolation, the agonizing loneliness that almost overwhelmed Jesus in the garden, has been overcome in the outpouring of Jesus's life. As one Eucharistic Prayer reminds us, '[Christ] opened wide His arms *for us* on the cross'.[42] He stretched them out to embrace the whole world: but in order to do that, He had to face all the horror of sin and suffering and humiliation, the horror of sheer nothingness. He had to bear the very worst that the world could do to reject the love of God. His love had to be strong enough to include the rejection, the betrayal, the cowardice of friends. His love had to be strong enough to include the racking pain, the mockery, the utter shame and degradation of crucifixion, 'the slave's punishment', reserved by Rome for rebels and runaways; agonizing and de-humanizing—and a public

---

[42] *Common Worship: Main Volume* (Church House Publishing, 2000), 188.

warning and deterrent to potential enemies of Rome. Christ's love for the world had to endure not only the physical pain but the total desolation of spirit expressed in that cry from the cross, "Eloi, Eloi, lama sabachthani?" (My God, my God, why have You forsaken me?). Only a love that could open its arms to embrace such a sense of desolation, of being utterly and completely abandoned, has power to heal the deepest wounds inflicted by human failure, human weakness, human sin. In Jesus Christ, crucified, dead and buried, God becomes the outcast of all, so that He can include all in His love.

> Who knows not Love, let him assay
> And taste that juice,

'Let him assay And taste'. God's love is something to be experienced. As the Psalmist wrote, 'O taste, and see, how gracious the Lord is' (Ps. 34:8 BCP).[43] We cannot earn God's love. We cannot, somehow, deserve it. We can only 'taste and see', open ourselves to the immeasurable stream flowing through the universe, accept it as God's free gift. We can only accept the delight and joy and wonder of being loved, loved by God, drawn out of the isolation and the nothingness in which sin seeks to entrap us, liberated into the light of God's presence. But, in accepting that love, in experiencing what it means to be loved by God, we find that we cannot simply be onlookers. Being loved involves us in loving. That can be costly. A later poet than George Herbert described the final end of our exploration into God's love as 'A condition of complete simplicity (costing not less than everything)'.[44] That scares us. We prefer to be comfortable. We would much rather be secure and safe. We prefer not to be involved in

---

[43] I have used the BCP translation here as, although Herbert would have known the King James translation, it is most likely in his daily Office that he would have used Coverdale's Psalter.

[44] T. S. Eliot, *Four Quartets*, 'Little Gidding', V.

the pain of other people, the pain of the world. We fear that *we* might get hurt.

However, it is in the pain, amid the fear, that the love of God is given flesh, as it is every time we step out beyond our desire for 'safety first', every time we lay ourselves open to the possibility of being hurt as we share in the pain of others. Every time we do that, we share in the pain of Christ. And, as we share in His pain, in His suffering, so we are enabled, with Him, to face and to overcome a little more of the pain of the world, a little more of the anguish and misery that results from human sin.

Through our baptism *we* have become identified with Christ, part of His body. We have committed ourselves to sharing in His death so that, as St Paul wrote to the Christians of Rome about twenty years after Jesus died, 'like as Christ was raised up from the dead by the glory of the Father, even so we also should walk in newness of life' (Rom. 6:4).

God gives us food to sustain us as we walk in that way. God feeds us with the bread and wine of the Eucharist. That bread and that wine are the tokens of love, tokens to be seen and touched and tasted. Through them God enables us to share His own life, His own love, uniting human beings across the boundaries that have been put up on the basis of differences in race, culture, nationality, age, ability, or wealth. The broken bread and the shared cup link us across time and space with all who have shared in the suffering and death of Jesus Christ and who share with us His risen life.

As we receive the bread and wine in the sacrament of Holy Communion, we receive Christ himself. We experience the reality of God's love for us, the reality that breaks down the barriers of sin and that sin can never destroy. The body, broken on the cross, the blood shed by the spear-thrust, are the evidences of God's love for His world. Love that is infinitely costly to God, and infinitely demanding of us.

To 'assay And taste that juice, which on the cross a pike Did set again abroach' is to discover the cost of love and the demand of love, the demand that we should love in our turn. The love, 'that liquor sweet and most divine, Which my God feels as blood; but I, as wine', not only draws us in to contemplate and adore. It also sends us out, to share in the costly work of loving, not on our own, and not relying on our own pitiful resources, but confident in the reality of Christ's victory over sin and death and trusting in the power of His Holy Spirit, the power that enables us to live and love and work to His praise and glory.

EASTER

Easter

Rise heart; thy Lord is risen. Sing His praise
                   Without delays,
Who takes thee by the hand, that thou likewise
                   With Him mayst rise:
That, as His death calcined thee to dust,
His life may make thee gold, and much more just.

Awake, my lute, and struggle for thy part
                   With all thy art.
The cross taught all wood to resound His name,
                   Who bore the same.
His stretchèd sinews taught all strings, what key
Is best to celebrate this most high day.

Consort both heart and lute, and twist a song
                   Pleasant and long:
Or since all music is but three parts vied
                   And multiplied;
O let thy blessed Spirit bear a part,
And make up our defects with His sweet art.

    I got me flowers to strew thy way;
    I got me boughs off many a tree:
    But thou wast up by break of day,
    And brought'st thy sweets along with thee.

The Sun arising in the East,
Though He give light, & th' East perfume;
If they should offer to contest
With thy arising, they presume.

Can there be any day but this,
Though many suns to shine endeavour?
We count three hundred, but we miss:
There is but one, and that one ever.

The final poem in this sequence is the two-part 'Easter'. This is one of half a dozen poems, including 'Christmas', 'The Holy Communion' and 'Good Friday', that change mood and metre in mid-poem. The poetic equivalent of a Bach prelude and fugue, perhaps?

It is appropriate to pause at the break, because the first part reminds us that Easter is not just a 'happy ending' to the story of a horrific miscarriage of justice. What happened to Jesus changes everything and transforms *us*, like a fierce fire burning away the dross to reveal the pure metal 'as His death calcined thee to dust, His life may make thee gold'. The death and resurrection of Jesus open up for everyone a new relationship with God and a new life that not even the death of our bodies can bring to an end. As the first stanza makes clear, this poem is not just about the resurrection of Jesus. It is also about our resurrection.

Sing His praise
Without delays,
Who takes thee by the hand, that thou likewise
With Him mayst rise:

Once again, there is the image of Christ taking sinful humanity 'by the hand' that we have found in 'Lent', the very first link in this chain of Herbert's poetry, and then in 'Love'. What was a hesitant aspiration at the beginning ('*Perhaps* my God, though He be far before, *May* turn and take me by the hand, and more: *May* strengthen my decays') became sacramental reality ('Love took my hand') and now, in this poem, the expression of our ultimate hope, as the risen Christ takes the poet's hand 'that thou likewise With Him mayst rise'.

That image suggests an intriguing possibility. From the end of the sixteenth century and well into the seventeenth there were growing contacts between the Church of England and the Eastern Orthodox Churches, particularly with the Ecumenical Patriarchate in Istanbul.[45] Cyril Lucaris, the Greek Orthodox Patriarch of Alexandria (1601–1620) and then of Constantinople (1620–1638), was well-disposed towards the Church of England. He was in correspondence with George Abbot, who was Archbishop of Canterbury (1611–1633), and one of Abbot's priests, Metrophanes Kritopoulos, was sent to study in Oxford from 1617 to 1624, around the same time that George Herbert was active in the academic life of Cambridge. Did Herbert meet Kritopoulos during his time in England? Had Herbert seen an Orthodox icon of the Resurrection?

It is an intriguing question: western depictions of Christ's rising from death show Him stepping out of the tomb in solitary triumph, as He does in, for example, the fresco by Piero della Francesca in Sansepolcro. That is very different from the way in which Eastern Orthodox depictions of the resurrection focus on Christ's descent to the abode of the dead. They show Him at the entrance to She'ol, or Hades, where He has already burst open the gates of death and trampled them underfoot. He is taking Adam and Eve by the hand and drawing them, and with them the patriarchs, the prophets, all the holy women and men of Israel's past, and behind them the whole of humanity, out from the realms of death into the eternal life of the kingdom of

---

[45] See Steven Runciman, *The Great Church in Captivity* (Cambridge University Press, 1968), chapter 7: 'The Anglican Experiment'.

heaven. The parallel with George Herbert's presentation of the Christ 'Who takes thee by the hand, that thou likewise With Him mayst rise' is quite striking.

The second stanza of the poem returns us to George Herbert's other great love, music. Earlier I highlighted his skill as a musician and his delight in music-making, and drew parallels between the poem 'Sin's Round' and the musical form of the 'round' or 'catch'. Here the poet, who was skilled at playing both the lute and the viol, uses the practicalities of getting sound out of a stringed instrument, and of making it heard among other instruments, to reflect on the image of Christ's sinews stretched taut against the wood of the cross.

> Awake, my lute, and struggle for thy part
> > With all thy art.
> The cross taught all wood to resound His name,
> > Who bore the same.
> His stretchèd sinews taught all strings, what key
> Is best to celebrate this most high day.

The opening words, 'Awake, my lute', echo the Psalms, especially (in view of what is to follow) Psalm 57:9, where the Psalmist declaims:

> My heart is fixed, O God, my heart is fixed:
> I will sing, and give praise.
> Awake up, my glory; awake, lute and harp:
> I myself will awake right early.

A very similar turn of phrase is found at the opening of Psalm 108:

> O God, my heart is fixed;
> I will sing and give praise, even with my glory.
> Awake, psaltery and harp:
> I myself will awake early.

I will praise thee, O Lord, among the people:
and I will sing praises unto thee among the nations.
For thy mercy is great above the heavens:
and thy truth reacheth unto the clouds. (Ps. 108:1–4)

The rest, though, is Herbert's own, although he returns to the Bible for detail. 'The cross taught all wood to resound His name, Who bore the same' has a rich ambiguity typical of George Herbert. Is that 'who' Jesus, described in the Passion Gospel on Good Friday, as bearing His own cross to the place of execution? Or is that 'who' the cross, personified, who bore the name of Jesus, and His designation as 'King of the Jews' in Latin, Greek and Hebrew, on the charge-sheet? The conceit that Jesus's 'stretched sinews', pulled taut by the nails and the force of gravity, provide the inspiration for the poet, as cat-gut pulled taut over the bridge of a lute provides music, is a powerful and, dare one say, quite a shocking one.

And then, *almost* like 'Sin's Round', we return to the poem's beginning in order to close this part of it:

Consort both heart and lute, and twist a song
                   Pleasant and long:
Or since all music is but three parts vied
                   And multiplied;
O let thy blessed Spirit bear a part,
And make up our defects with His sweet art.

A 'consort' in Elizabethan and Jacobean music is a group of instruments, either a 'whole consort', in which all the instruments are of the same type, usually viols, or recorders, or else one that is 'broken' or 'mixed', in which different kinds of instrument, plucked strings and bowed strings, or strings and wind instruments, play (or 'consort') together. Consort music was a popular form of domestic music-making in better-off homes. Composers such as John Cooper, alias Giovanni Coprario, and Alfonso

Ferrabosco (or George Herbert's younger contemporaries, John Jenkins and William Lawes) met the demand for it in the same way that, in a later age, Haydn or Mozart would provide trios and quartets in which their musically gifted friends and patrons could enjoy participating. Here we have a 'broken consort' of heart and lute, providing the basis for such music. Given that the lute is regularly used as a metaphor for true feelings in the sixteenth and seventeenth centuries, it is likely that Herbert is praying that intellect, symbolized by the heart, and emotion, symbolized by the lute, may join together in the praises of the risen Christ.

But, as Herbert points out, all music is based on the three notes, the triad, that make up a common chord. A 'chest of viols', which could be an important item of furniture for well-off, musically-inclined families, would normally hold three sizes of instrument: treble (usually two), tenor (two or three) and bass (two or one). So, where is Herbert to find the third voice, to add to his heart and his lute? At this point, it is tempting to go back to Mr Herbert's method of catechizing, as we learned it in our exploration of 'Redemption'. If 'all music is but three parts', what else do Christians naturally think of as a triad? The answer, surely, is God. The word from which we derive triad, τριας, is the Greek equivalent of the Latin *trinitas*, the English trinity. So, Herbert asks God:

> O let thy blessed Spirit bear a part,
> And make up our defects with His sweet art.

Herbert prays for the help of God's Spirit in making and performing the heart's song. That song forms the second part of this poem. And what a song it is! Ralph Vaughan Williams was so captivated by its simplicity that in *Five Mystical Songs* he set it separately from the first part of the poem.

In form, the song is an *aubade*, a love-song to be sung at dawn by the lover outside the window of the beloved. So far, as often with Herbert, so apparently conventional. But it is not conventional at all. This *aubade* is not to be sung outside the beloved's window. It was intended to be sung, presumably, outside the entrance to His tomb. And, as usual, the 'simplicity' of George Herbert's language is packed with echoes and resonances. In those simple words 'I got me flowers to strew thy way; I got me boughs off many a tree' he reminds us of the entry of Jesus into Jerusalem (Matt. 21:8, Mark 11:8, John 12:13), when the crowds spread their cloaks and cut tree branches to lay in His path as a mark of honour. He reminds us, too, of the courageous women who came 'at early dawn' (Luke 24:1); 'while it was still dark' (John 20:1). They came bringing their 'sweets': not Easter eggs, but spices to anoint the corpse of Jesus. But He was 'up by break of day': the tomb was empty. "Why seek ye the living among the dead?" asked the mysterious men in shining garments. "He is not here, but is risen." (Luke 24:5–6).

That is where the incontestable glory and wonder of Easter begins: with three startled women. In St Mark's account of Easter morning they flee from the tomb in terror and amazement, running away from a mystery they do not understand, an emptiness that is somehow full of life, and the missing corpse of a person whose living presence we experience in our midst two thousand years later. "Why seek ye the living among the dead?" ask the men at the tomb. George Herbert asks a rather different question: 'Can there be any day but this?' Easter marks the first day of God's new creation, God's eternal day. However dark things may appear, we live, always, in the light of the resurrection. We walk with the risen Jesus in newness of life, 'dead unto sin', as St Paul wrote to the first Christian communities in Rome, 'but alive unto God through Jesus Christ our Lord' (Rom. 6:11). As St Augustine of Hippo is said to have told his flock three and a half centuries later,

We are an Easter people, and Alleluia is our song.

SLG PRESS PUBLICATIONS

CONTEMPLATIVE POETRY SERIES

CP1	*Amado Nervo: Poems of Faith and Doubt*	trans. John Gallas (2021)
CP2	*Anglo-Saxon Poets: The High Roof of Heaven*	trans. John Gallas (2021)
CP3	*Middle English Poets: Where Grace Grows Ever Green*	
		trans. and ed. John Gallas (2021)
CP4	*The Voice Inside our Home*	Edward Clarke (2022)

VESTRY GUIDES

VG1	*The Visiting Minister: How to Welcome Visiting Clergy to Your Church*	
		Paul Monk (2021)
VG2	*Help! No Minister! or Please Take the Service*	Paul Monk (2022)

slgpress.co.uk